BALLADS TO THE BURNING TWINS

THE COMPLETE SONG LYRICS OF THE DEATHRAY BRADBURYS

ALEXANDER ZELENYJ

Ballads To The Burning Twins:
The Complete Song Lyrics Of The Deathray Bradburys
Publication Date: 01 November 2014
Copyright Alexander Zelenyj

Photography copyright Elizabeth Walker

Cover Art copyright David Rix

ISBN: 978-1-908125-35-4

www.eibonvalepress.co.uk

CONTENTS:

The Deathray Bradburys Discography   8

Foreword   15

The Deathray Bradburys: A Brief History, An Eternal Mystery   17

The Songs   29

The 7" Singles   47

Other Songs   57

The Deathray Bradburys Discography

Full-Length LP:

There Is A Place (Saucer Records 1998; Re-Issued Ryko Records, 2008)

1. *Somewhere, Someone Heard*
2. *First Colony*
3. *Our Star Medicine*
4. *Light Of Sirius (A)*
5. *New Family*
6. *Black Lash Of Lucifer*
7. *The Twins*
8. *A Summer Night A.D.*
9. *Maria 16*
10. *Roads Through Big Black*
11. *If There Is A Lord*
12. *Robert The Mighty*
13. *Fortress*

7" Records:

Peace-Star For The Lost Sixteen (Punk Salvation Records, 1998)

Side A:

1. *Peace-Star For The Lost Sixteen*

Side B:

2. *Black In The Heart Of Man*

The Lara Trilogy (Saucer Records, 1998)

Side A:

1. *The Mornings Lara Died*
2. *Lara, Born Again*

Side B:

3. *Lara, We Love You Good*

Dark Earth (Saucer Records, 1999)

Side A:

1. Dark Earth

Side B:

2. Secret Sister (Light Of Sirius C)

Secret Paths To Secret Places (Coordinates) (Secret Records, 1999)

Side A:

1. Secret Paths To Secret Places (Coordinates) (Part 1)

Side B:

2. Secret Paths To Secret Places (Coordinates) (Part II)

Assorted known material, taken from various archival & bootleg sources (omitting four known live bootlegged songs of exceptionally poor quality whose lyrics cannot be deciphered).:

1. *Untitled* (live track only, circa 1998)

2. *Light Of Sirius (B)* (demo, circa 1997)

3. *Untitled II* (live track only, circa 2000, commonly known among fans as *Heaven, 1997*)

4. *Untitled III* (demo, year unknown; commonly known among fans as *Fuck The Demon*)

5. *The Monitors* (demo, 1998)

6. *Mighty Son* (demo, circa 2000)

7. *County Road 26 To Infinity* (demo, circa 1997)

For those who need this energy.

*"Somewhere a band is playing
Oh listen, oh listen, that tune!
If you learn it you'll dance on forever
In June...
and yet June...
and more...June...
And Death will be dumb and not clever
And Death will lie silent forever
In June and yet June and more June"*

- Ray Bradbury, from *"Somewhere A Band Is Playing"*

Foreword

Where have they led us? Where is our family now as you read this? Where this promised silver light and greenest summer? Where are the Deathray Bradburys and their great seeking caravan?

  In a good place.
  But also here, in these words in your hands.
  Let them in if you need to.

Alexander Zelenyj & Elizabeth Walker
Windsor, Ontario, August 31, 2000

- This preface was found attached to the type-written collection of transcribed song lyrics — as well as the myriad photographs by Elizabeth Walker — that make up the bulk of this volume. The manuscript was discovered in Windsor, Ontario in the days following the mass disappearance of the Deathray Bradburys and 225 of their followers.

The Deathray Bradburys: A Brief History, An Eternal Mystery

Good evening! And welcome thee to this night when the skies and Heaven above shall open wide and bleed down and down and down their light and love unto this soil, and into the red, red, red, red world below! And in this middle-country, oh, in this right-here right-now lieth you and us! And you are beautiful, and we are the Deathray Bradburys, and this world – oh, this sad, lonely, wicked, vengeful *world – oh, she is no match for us! For tonight we are gathered here to offer you celestial salvation from your woes! The Twins are burning and the Twins are calling! Paradise awaits! Join us, brothers and sisters –* this is our night!

- from the anonymous singer's introduction to the final Deathray Bradburys performance, August 31, 2000 (Green 2)

555:

The binary star Sirius, also known as the "dog star" or "Big Dog" because of its place in the constellation Canis Major, is the brightest star in the sky and has therefore long been revered by peoples throughout the world. Its very name comes from the Greek word "seirius", meaning "scorching" or "searing", its brilliance and prominence in the sky having earned it a long-standing place in occult symbolism and the mythologies of some of the world's most pre-eminent empires. The ancient Egyptian's entire mythology and religious system, for example, revolved around Sirius, owing largely to the fact that their ancient astronomers observed that the Nile flooded whenever the sun was aligned with the star, providing fertility to the land. Known as the Nile Star, Sirius was said to be the birthplace of their most prominent deities, including Osiris, Isis, Seth and Horus, and its rising formed the basis of the Egyptian's calendar (Sutton 101).

The mystery of humankind's connection to Sirius deepened in the twentieth century. In 1931 French explorers and anthropologists Marcel Griaule and Germaine Dieterlen first made contact with the Dogon, a small reclusive tribe living in Mali, West Africa. The anthropologists discovered that the Dogon's folklore included a rich and elaborate mythology revolving around the star Sirius. This mythology was based on information said to have been passed down through generations as far back as 3200 B.C., and included an extensive and inexplicable knowledge of the science underlying the star. With advances in European and Western astronomy came proof that much of the Dogon people's knowledge relating to Sirius was accurate, a seemingly miraculous fact considering their Stone Age society's complete lack of scientific discipline (Sutton 105).

How, without scientific equipment of any kind, could the Dogon have known that a smaller star, now recognized as Sirius B and invisible to the naked eye, orbits Sirius, that its orbital cycle is exactly 50 years long, and that it rotates on its own axis? It was only in the 1950s, after all, that a telescope was developed that was powerful enough to see Sirius B, and it wasn't until 1970 that it was first photographed. Further, the Dogon showed knowledge of Sirius B's immense density and classification as a white dwarf star – this primitive people named the star *Po Tolo* (Tolo in the Dogon language means "star" while "Po" is the smallest seed known to their society) and referred to it as the "heaviest star", describing it as being "white" in colour (Nalton 125).

The Dogon also claimed knowledge of a third star orbiting behind Sirius B – they called it *Emme Ya*, and its existence was conclusively proven as recently as 1995, when French scientists Daniel Benest and J.L. Duvent detected motions in the Sirius system that they attributed to a possible third star. It is now commonly referred to as Sirius C and remains a point of intense interest for astronomers (Zukal 15).

The Dogon said their knowledge of astronomy was long ago passed to them by the *Nommos*, an extraterrestrial race of intelligent amphibious beings sent as emissaries from Sirius. Descriptions of the *Nommos* can be equated to mermen and mermaids of ancient legend, and can also be found in Sumerian, Babylonian and Accadian myths. Most accounts of the tale describe these beings as having arrived in an ark-like craft, amid great thunder and fire. Their purpose, according to the Dogon, was to act as spiritual saviours for the human race, bestowing their metaphysical and astronomical knowledge to those who would listen. For this reason the *Nommos* were also called the "Teachers" and the "Monitors". The Dogon claimed that the *Nommos* would some day return to Earth, taking control of its waters and ruling the world, in this way making the world "clean again". It was also said that the *Nommos* make periodic visits to the Earth, and reward followers for their devotion by bringing them back to Sirius, which the Dogon believe to be a heavenly realm or paradise (Nalton, 130 – 132).

Over the years it has become accepted that the Dogon could not have acquired their vast scientific knowledge of Sirius without contact with a technologically advanced civilization – whether this scientific knowledge was terrestrial or extraterrestrial in origin has never been conclusively determined, although there is a great deal of evidence in support of the latter. The tribe's inexplicable and astonishingly advanced scientific knowledge is given incontrovertible proof in the form of a 400-year-old Dogon artefact which bears a clear depiction of the Sirius configuration, as well as the Dogon's ceremonial celebration of Sirius A and B's cycle, a ritual dating back to the 13th century.

Sirius continues to enthral people the modern world over, as it has since before times of written record. This long and rich history has infused the unprecedented events revolving around the Deathray Bradburys and their alleged spiritual connection to the binary star with an added scope and an ever deepening mystery.

666:

The enigma of The Deathray Bradburys has endured over a decade, and could be compared to sifting through the ruins of a once thriving civilization that inexplicably vanished without a trace, leaving a proverbial ghost town for bewildered fans and researchers to examine and re-examine and speculate over in its wake.

Very little is known about the Deathray Bradburys. The seminal band's career was short-lived: the five-piece formed sometime between 1995 and 1997 and concluded their recording and touring existence in late summer 2000. Although their place of origin isn't known for certain, it's speculated to be somewhere in the greater Windsor-Essex County area of South Western Ontario, due to the fact of their playing an exorbitantly large number of performances within this geographic region (though the band did tour throughout other parts of the country in their later days, as well as into the United States). The most prominent cities frequented by the band included Windsor, Chatham, London, Hamilton, Kingston, and Toronto, and smaller towns in the vicinity of Windsor, such as Belle River, Comber, Woodslee, Harrow, Leamington and Kingsville, among others (Warner 23).

Stylistically, they played a raw and minimalist form of garage rock, with a heavy nod to the frenetically-paced, three-chord punk rock of the late 1970s and a melodic sensibility reminiscent of 1950s bubblegum pop and doo-wop. They precociously merged this with an overtly psychedelic guitar and keyboard influence – along with typically reverb-drenched vocals – which embellished the band with a distinctly spacey quality in keeping with their overall cosmic aesthetic. They were famed for their unabashed embracing of B-movie inspired imagery – each band member wore retro/pseudo-futuristic silver costumes and masks (complete with antennae, goggles and, occasionally, wings!) so that no one ever learned their identities. Interestingly enough, the band members never disclosed their names, either real or stage names, preferring the mystery that came with total anonymity. They likewise refused to do interviews, although admittedly any noteworthy print publications that would have been interested in giving the then little-known band coverage were few and far between; the only forums known to have written about the band were fanzine-type publications with very limited circulation, most likely passing from person to person at live performances, through small independent record shops, or via other underground channels (Green, 30 – 34).

Yet the Deathray Bradburys would become most famous in underground circles – and ultimately to the rest of the world – for their lyrical fixation, an obsessive focus revolving around themes of escape from a decadent, increasingly violent and racist world to a paradisiacal place of salvation. The idea of this haven, at first glance a seemingly fictitious creation, was repeatedly reinforced as authentic by the group's proselytizing on-stage banter and the recurring mini-essays and poetry-like texts found as liner notes in their recordings, describing the tenets of this belief, as well as a timeline establishing a set date for a planned exodus from Earth to this paradise. Going to a Deathray Bradburys concert was much like attending an evangelical sermon, complete with a self-proclaimed prophet – in this case the band's lead singer/front man, delivering impassioned between-song orations imploring the band's followers to embrace the higher power of which they sang – and throngs of spellbound followers in rapture of the spectacle unfolding before them.

The basic story as proposed by the Deathray Bradburys in their cryptic lyrics described a future mass exodus that they themselves were to lead (exactly how the band came about this knowledge was hinted at but never fully disclosed). Those chosen to accompany them were individuals with a deep emotional and spiritual need to escape their own personal woes, and more generally the misery inherent in life on Earth. As the story went, those who followed the band and believed in their promise of salvation would likewise be saved alongside their musical heroes, ultimately to be transported – some believed spiritually while others believed physically – from their lives and into this heavenly paradise among the stars: the "light" of the Sirius binary star system. The group's lyrics speak of Sirius in fanatically reverential terms, and have a foundation based in the historical and mythological roots relating to the star.

The exodus was scheduled to take place, for reasons once again apparently known only to the band itself, on the final night of August in the year 2000. Debate continues concerning the means by which this "ascension" was intended to occur – many analyses of the group's lyrics and literature speculate that mass suicide represented the medium through which the salvation promised by the group was purported to take place, as evidenced by recurring references to the drinking of "potions" of ambiguous "energy". Suicide is indeed a recurring theme throughout the band's body of work, and specifically the repeated allusions to the "freedom" it provided from unrelenting misery and sadness. The song "Robert The Mighty", for example, seems to be an ode to pulp writer Robert E. Howard, elevating his life and subsequent suicide to divine proportions in accordance with the Deathray Bradburys' belief in the transcendence afforded those who took themselves from the mortal world ("The New Seekers: The Cult of the Deathray Bradburys").

In "County Road 26 To Infinity" tribute is paid to "the angels Boreal and Wood", a worshipful reference to both cult leader Michael Boreal, the founder of the Sirius Group who led his disciples in a mass suicide on the island of Magahatti (Murray, 57 – 59); as well as James William Wood, infamous for his abduction of the fifteen women who would come to be known as the Essex Fifteen, each a victim of forced or assisted suicide (debate still rages as to which) and promised ascension to a heavenly realm: Sirius. Members of the so-called Essex Fifteen are likewise mentioned throughout the DB canon, such as in the songs "Peace-Star For The Lost Sixteen" and "Maria 16" – a reference to the youngest victim of the Essex Fifteen, Maria Reed; the numeral appended to the name in the latter echoing the title of the former, and signifying the band's sympathetic belief that Wood himself should be included in the group of suicide victims, bringing their number to sixteen victims rather than solely the fifteen women ("Onwards To Heaven: The Story of the Essex Fifteen").

Topically, the band wove an eclectic number of subjects within the greater tapestry of the recurring and unifying themes of suicide and escape from a violent world. References to lilies recur throughout the band's lyrics, providing a link to the inexplicable phenomenon of this flower species growing in abundance at the site of the Essex Fifteen group suicide in Essex County, Ontario. The flower became symbolic of the band, and fans attending their concerts would reputedly wear them in their hair or throw them onto the stage during performances ("Star Children: The Story of the Deathray Bradburys"). Constant comparisons are made in the band's lyrics between the sullied and decadent modern world of the city to the purity of times long past, the beauty and splendour of bucolic environments versus the dangers of the modern world and its insistence on (often dangerous) technological advances; as well as the contrast between the innocence and wonder of childhood and its loss in adulthood. These ideas draw a neat line to the band's namesake, Ray Bradbury, much of whose work delves into these very themes (Warner 15).

Interestingly, given the Deathray Bradburys' quasi-cult/religious stance, their lyrics make no effort to deny the existence of God or Satan, but rather suggest that their own prophetic visions offer their disciples an alternative to both. Biblical references throughout their literature to the Devil, angels and giant figures reminiscent of the Nephilim (the Biblical giants said to be a product of the union between the sons of God and the daughters of men) suggest an acceptance of the tenets posited by a variety of organized religions, while simultaneously giving equal credence to subjects rooted firmly in scientific foundations and ancient alchemy – these include the scientific experiments and aspirations of trailblazing inventor and physicist Nikola Tesla; the age of the dinosaurs, an epoch spoken of in romantic terms for its absence of humankind, often described as a violent and ruining force; interstellar phenomena such as stars, worm-holes, and space travel; and more arcane sciences, such as ancient numerology, alchemy, and occult mysticism.

Mythological subject matter recurs in the group's lyrics as well, ranging from allusions to the Greek myth of Icarus to ancient African lore, with the story of Tombanik, an active volcano long said in the folklore of the region to be inhabited by a god fallen from the sky. Interestingly, these myths involve themes of flight and celestial phenomena, both themes seen elsewhere in the band's writing. References to the sea and ocean abound in their lyrics as well – the Greek sea-god Proteus appears in several songs, as well as direct references to the amphibious sea-dwelling *Nommos* and their promise to reclaim and purify the Earth's oceans (Green 205).

Aesthetically speaking, the Deathray Bradburys evoked a unique combination of imagery in their lyrics, ranging from the cosmic to the bucolic representing the positive side of the spectrum, and the modern world/society – specifically the city – as its antithesis. This, and the need (and means) to escape from a world too often rife with emotional suffering and anguish, marked the foundation of the band's message.

Fantastic as the premise of the group's promised ascension sounds, its appeal to a contingent of the underground music community was profound: fans of the Deathray Bradburys treated the band as some religious devotees treat their faith, with absolute conviction and a dedication bordering on fanaticism. This lyrical subject matter – as well as the prayerful, angry and outraged manner with which it was often expressed – found particular appeal among disaffected youth, as it offered both a sympathetic voice while speaking very clearly to an end of suffering and a promise of rescue from a downtrodden existence. For this reason the band began drawing increasingly loyal crowds to their concerts at small bars and all-ages community centres even before the release of their debut album, sowing the seeds of their future legacy. Rather judiciously, the band omitted certain details of their invented story, lending it a deliciously cryptic and enticing air that allowed for fans to fill in gaps as they liked.

Knowledge of the Deathray Bradburys' seeming sincerity in the proclamations they made grew through word-of-mouth to define the band's agenda, setting them apart from their peers, as well as any rock and roll groups that came before them or have come since. The group's entire catalogue – comprised of a single full-length album entitled *There Is A Place* (self-released on Saucer Records in July 1998, reissued as a tenth anniversary special edition in 2008 by Ryko Records) as well as several obscure 7" singles releases and countless bootleg recordings – reflect this thematic focus, occasionally with gleeful simplicity and vulgarity appropriate to their punk rock roots, but more often with a breathtaking poeticism paralleling their literary inspirations and worthy of the grand and grave subject matter of which they sang. The Deathray Bradburys' wildly eclectic stylistic approach ran the gamut from anthemic rally calls directing their followers and praising their collective spiritual beliefs, to impassioned tributes to their literary and other influences, to poignant philosophical dissertations on the nature of living in and seeking haven from a difficult and uncompromising world.

Some have argued that this obsession and seductive rhetoric made the band as much a cult based on persuasive charismatic manipulation of its adherents as they were a group of musicians. Whatever their agenda, the band's musical prowess can't be ignored. With a variety of tightly-crafted, deceptively simple pop-inflected anthems drawing influences from a variety of genres and styles to their credit they represented something of an anomaly in the music world:

a garage band of immense talent and originality whose chief objective was not only light years removed from the lofty goals of fame and fortune which so many other bands aspire to attain; but the purported fulfillment of spiritual ideals they pursued to the utter neglect of a burgeoning career. In the process they provided a source of spiritual hope for their small but madly devoted fan base.

777:

It remains unknown what became of the members of the underground band the Deathray Bradburys following their final performance at the Coach And Horses in Windsor, Ontario on Thursday, August 31st 2000. For all intents and purposes, the band – along with a reported thirty local missing persons linked to the event, and one hundred ninety-five people from throughout other areas of the province – quite literally fell off the face of the Earth, coinciding with the date set for their preordained, fictitious(?) exodus. An extensive province-wide search was undertaken throughout the months following, yielding no clues whatsoever as to the whereabouts of those missing. The case, a decade on, remains unresolved while debate continues as to whether this represents one of the most elaborately staged mass-scale hoaxes in history, or something else entirely. As a result of these unexplained circumstances the band's ever-growing cult status remains assured, as well as the legacy of mystery and romance – and grandly evocative music – they've left behind. It goes without saying that the group's body of lyrics continues to be scrutinized.

In positing theories as to the whereabouts of the Deathray Bradburys and their missing followers, perhaps it's best – if exceedingly romantic – to conclude with the enigmatic yet seemingly prophetic words of the band itself:

"There is a place
Far beyond all of this despair
We promise you, friends:
There is a place for us all."

- from the song *First Colony*

First published in *Underground Tracks* Volume 1, Issue 252, November 2010.
Author: A.B. Sossi

Works Cited

"The New Seekers: The Cult Of The Deathray Bradburys" *Strange World: The Complete Second Season*. Prod. Brian Adamson. Forbidden Home Entertainment, 2002. DVD.

Green, Alec. *In Search Of The Deathray Bradburys*. New York, NY: Dawn Star Press, 2012. Print.

Murray, Dennis. *Away From Night And Into Light: The Ascension of the Sirius Group*. Secaucus, NJ: Sky Books, 2002. Print.

Nalton, Philip. *The Dogon And Other Prophetic Peoples*. Windsor, ON: Forest Glade Press, 1983. Print.

Star Children: The Story Of The Deathray Bradburys. Prod. Henry Nissell. Spotlight Productions, 2010. DVD.

Sutton, Elaine. *Tribes Of The Ancient Past*. Gainesville, KY: Sand Press, 1975. Print.

Onwards To Heaven: The Story Of The Essex Fifteen. Prod. Travis, Dorothy. Rose City Productions, 2002. DVD.

Warner, Georgio. *Star Family: What Happened To The Deathray Bradburys And Their Followers?* London, UK: Random House, 2010. Print.

Zukal, Daniel. *Astronomy For The New Millennium*. Toronto, ON: Seer Press, 2010. Print.

THE SONGS

THERE IS A PLACE (LP)

Somewhere, Someone Heard

A girl walking home was found by a Devil-man
The evil happened in a field
silver with flowers and the moon
behind a gas station
deep after midnight

She prayed for the first time that night

Somewhere, someone heard

She found she could sleep
Her dreams were filled with light
These were Summer dreams…

They cradled her until she woke

Her days grew haunted:
her prayers grew stronger

Somewhere, someone heard

Sweet Katherine's ghosts lived strong though too
and clamoured to be let out:
she cut her wrists open

Somewhere, someone heard

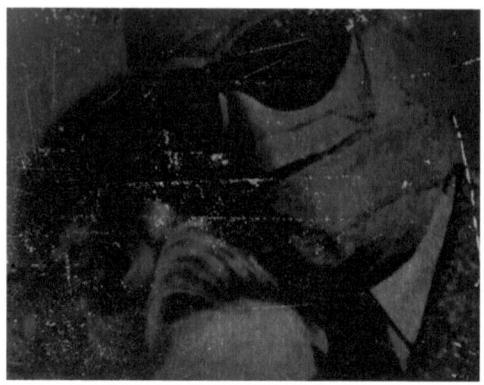

First Colony

Your gods went away.

~

In the east
the vacuum is warmed by their light:
Twins like home-fires in the cold

There is a place
Far beyond all of this despair
We promise you, friends:
There is a place for us all.

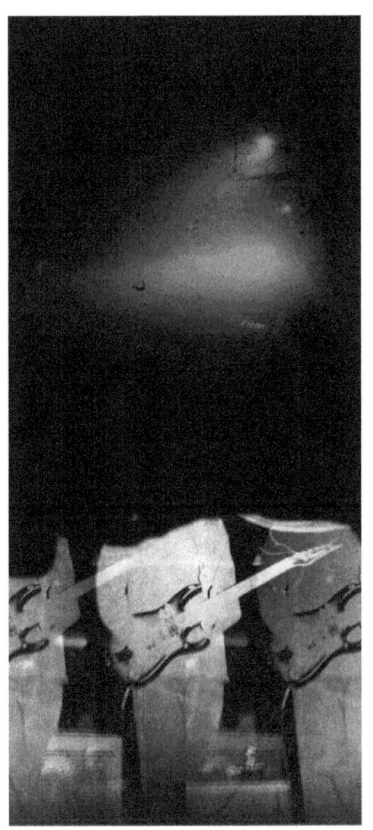

Our Star Medicine

R is for Rocket
for S is for Space
for always something wicked this way comes
So brother join sister, the night draws near
The final eve of August in 2000

Spike our needle high
and set down far from all this

A house exists for us
where fear never lived
Our medicine for melancholy

Light Of Sirius (A)

Canis Major rules the night
tonight as tomorrow
as a million years ago

Once dinosaurs roamed free of men:
A thought to dream to

But there is Peace
It is a fortress
in the Twins who rule the night

The Songs

New Family

Brothers and sisters, the world was bright and kind
It's all we ever knew
Then in a great darkness badness was born
And inside a night it brought it to us, too
Brothers, we can jump away
Sisters, this dark isn't spun too tight
O they, they are the ones we hate
O they, they are the ones we hate

Join you us, brothers and sisters
We the new tribe bringing back the light
We the new family flying straight into the light

Black Lash Of Lucifer

To have never known?
Or to have been bound in Paradise
until savage Sunday saw the golden embrace cut?

Of course we would take the same paths of pain
if given the choice again, and again, and again...
This is who we are.

We're everywhere in this lotus dream
These tangled streets are heavy with us,
honeycombing the slumped buildings, too
We need and fear the same havens
while drawing light inside of mirrors
But it's everywhere,
the Black Lash of Lucifer:
our loneliness

The Twins

Darling, we have only to live through the cold years
At the end of them, a Summer night

Dog-star and God-star pulsing
The hearts of Summer in winter's body
Big brother and invisible Po Tolo
We may name them as we wish
We may call on them as we need

Spitfire and destroyer sleeping in ocean tomb
the submerged skeleton armies dreaming fitfully too
These are the ragged new cities of the fish.
Fear not: the waters will be divine again

But darling, we have only to live through the cold years
At the end of them, Twins burning
in the cold miles we've been moving through
since the day we were born

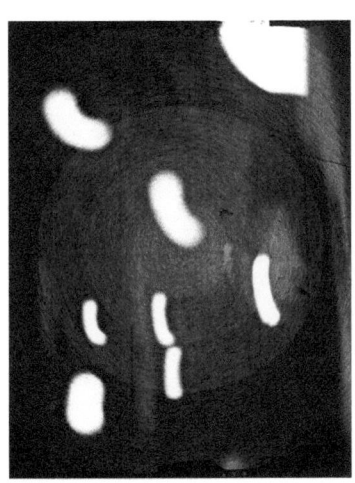

A Summer Night A.D.

*Hounds from below and hawks from above
meet in this dirty middle-ground
But there's nothing to fear: we're leaving
this place dead of light and love*

Even the oldest ghosts burn away in the exodus

*August, hedge us in your arms
Sirius, enfold us in your Summer*

*Somewhere an ancient lake lies waiting
to cleanse the blessed swimmers*

*You
and us.*

The Songs

Maria 16

Maria 16 – the boys all loved her
Maria 16 – the men all burned her

Oh, the things people do
Oh, the things people do

But it's okay, Maria:
you have a family now.

Roads Through Big Black

Harmony and Delores and the sisters thirteen,
picked flowers with brother sixteen, too
Their toil was a joy
They were rewarded with wings

<~ Nazca and her ancient lines
We waited even then ~>

The flyer flies forever in old Copán

It took this many long hard years too.
If only we'd known
what Roads lied ahead

And after the Maze: Home.

If There Is A Lord

If there is a Lord
we know where He resides

If there is a Lord
He was known long ago
The Dogon were visited
and later Osiris inspired from the sun

"O Nommos, teach us,"
the old ones cried

The Big Dog the Sun
The silver disc wheeling

If there is a Lord
we each of us can be Him.

Robert The Mighty

Robert he knew
much of good and savagery,
lands pure and cities sullied
Robert he knew to seize his crown young

"Goodbye mother."
He raised his gun bravely

Robert, he is King
And his Kingdom is Forever

Fortress

People are wicked and people are shit
but there stand walls too mighty for enemies to breach

There stand walls too mighty for enemies to breach.

THE 7" SINGLES

Peace-Star For The Lost Sixteen

Where did the Essex women go?
Summoned like the tides by the moon
But where did those county women go?
Lost like a whisper in the waving wheat
But people ask "Where did the pretty girls go?"
Away like smoke on a midnight wind
But where and where did the Essex Fifteen go?
Like bonfires they finally were put out

Why did the Essex women go?

They say no one knows why
they let Jimmy put them in the sky

And where did your great thief go?
Where's Jimmy Wood this lonely night?
No one knows, no one knows,
Maybe Jimmy burns in the sky now, too
Maybe Jimmy isn't the thief at all

Listen in your heart and hear his words ring true:
the Essex Fifteen are in a better place,
a kinder place after all
The Essex Fifteen are burning good, Jim
Left their ghosts behind to haunt Lily Wood
We're headed lightwards, too
to meet the quiet county's girls
On your peace-star we'll gather again
to pick starflowers every day

Jim Wood and the captive women
All Sixteen of them finally freed
Take care of them, Jimmy
Take care of our lilies
Garden the sky, Jimmy
Brighten the night
Tend to the night, Jimmy
tonight and every night

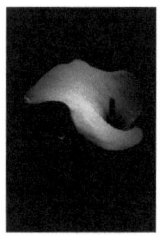

Black In The Heart Of Man

"I love you un-fatherly."
His kisses were black.

Evil in a man's heart
Love in the lights of the east

"Love is the cure for all the great sickness,"
the angel said.
Fly with us:
a murder of the mighty-winged

Through wormhole eye
Through black hole mouth
this cosmic caravan drifts untiring

Like two eyes
Like two candles
to burn away the night you should never have known.
to burn away the night that made you old.

The Lara Trilogy:

The Mornings Lara Died

Deep in the mornings
was when Lara died

The A.M. miles were long
A young county chute mastered citywards
and left to perfume the new day alone.

Lara, Born Again

Lara she heard a song
and Lara she danced for the first time
and for the first time she knew no world
shaking under her feet

Now we're strong.
Ghosts fear us.

"Follow the ships that come not back," he told her
Follow those ships that come not back

She'll never come back again.

Lara, We Love You Good

Pretty Lara, you may finally sleep
where worry has no home.
Devil-Gods left hungry behind you
to scuff the world with cloven hoof

Your dreams are un-plagued.

−

Far away,
a lily grows overtop her grave.

Dark Earth

On a morning in September
young Henry woke
to find shadows eating the sun
In these long hours before school began
Henry learned his first lesson of the day

It was a dark Earth that held him
when most he wanted to float away

"Fuck," he learned the word and spoke it
like a bullet every day.
"Paradise," he learned and dropped it
a new bomb into brighter nights
"Death," he said, and "Energy"
They became his weapons too.

Young Henry was old then
trudged the miles to school alone
Friends he didn't make
with eyes only for steps away
Until he heard a song
that put his eyes with his hope
patrolling the stone clouds

Then summer returned
and oh, he'd never believed it could!
And although it was a Dark Earth that held him
Henry beat his new wings to float away

Secret Sister (Light Of Sirius C)

Seven Gods
Six Devils
Five men
This is evil alchemy

We your tribe, we share with you secrets
of little hidden sister
Emme Ya some named you
We call you C for the deep sea
Proteus and his fish of infinity

It only seems right
given the Fifteen disappeared
for two brothers to share the dark miles
with little sister,
secret but so strong

Let us drink to all three
With these our cups filled of energy

Two make a family
But three make a tribe

Secret Paths To Secret Places (Coordinates)

In old Africa's dark heart
a jewel in angry Tombanik's mouth

Under sands in pyramidal shadow
Sothis scorched then too

There! The new Martians reflected
in Ray's canal waters

Oh Philip in the light,
flowing all around

With dreams of Utopia Nikola laboured alone,
light and energy without limit
and a road to Mars too
during lightning storms he spoke not to himself
but to friends far and away

The Group hails these men out of time
We will all celebrate in the light

while here a forest of impossible lilies
blooms from a holy sky

These are the secret coordinates
Our family will gather
The new tribe will strike out bravely

Drink this nectar
This potion gives wings

Alezabeh, rejoice!
Your castle awaits

Proteus, take us in your sea-chariot
Proteus, take us deep and away and to a good day

A good day.

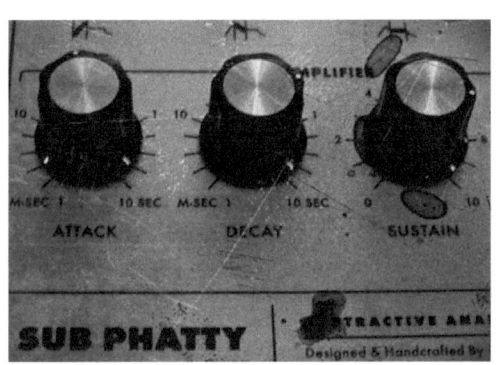

OTHER SONGS

Untitled I

But they'll die too
and we will live after them

Forever

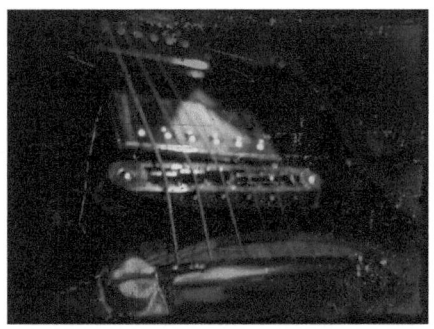

Light Of Sirius (B)

Out past this hungry house
with its spirit-fingers deep in you
Away from a city's demon-trick faces
and false homes hiding Death alive in the cracks
Light years from murder abounding
in a burning raping hexing Earth
Escapees from a broken place
where men call men nigger and faggot,
slave and ant and nothing more than this,
where to cleanse the land with fire
is to will some be burned by gods

His hands were pits, and his and his and his.
Hush: put your thoughts far away, little rabbit

We gather here a lost tribe of the Godless good

Into the heart of Sirius we'll go
Into the heart of the light we'll go
On silver wings we'll go

Untitled II, commonly known among fans as Heaven, 1997

First seen in 1862
first caught in 1970
you found us: it was 1997

We'd never believed in Heaven
until 1997
Face to face with the 777

Today we look past poison times
dead sisters and their spectral woe
broken brothers salt-watering the lily-worms
mothers empty as your father's churches

"An angel flying through the midst of Heaven
saying with a loud voice, Woe, woe, woe, to the inhabiters of the Earth"

It's been coming since the first knife hewn
from fateful bone or stone

Everyone is dead inside.

Now we wrathchildren dream of True Heaven

Untitled III, commonly known among fans as Fuck The Demon

Run away with us
Fuck the Demon better than it's raped you
Escape through potion or blood
Elope by the left hand of this Old Science

Do you feel them?
Do you feel their pull?
Do you feel their light?
Do you feel their warmth?
Do you feel their strength?

Over there it's always Summer

Drink.

You're free

The Monitors

The old Teachers,
our Angels of history,
Masters of our seas
and the Twins' tranquility

Is there a third?
The lucky will learn

What do you think of us
taken as a whole?
Read us as a book,
show us where we failed

A man sees a monster,
a woman, frothing Devil
but here a child brutalized like clockwork
No: the Teachers are beautiful,
only sometimes their light burns too strong

We must pity the men whose war-hearts can't see

We must be grateful for Them watching over you and me

Mighty Son

*"Then up from the marsh,
under misty cliffs
Grendel came walking;
He bore God's wrath"*

*Brother Grendel,
we understand you
Their music is not ours,
Hounded and hunted no way to live*

*Come away
Climb this one last silver slope
Bring your beautiful mother too
Together peace will be your company
long after Geat and Dane
have wept their last
for your mighty deeds*

County Road 26 To Infinity

*County Road 26
a gate and portal between the flower-fall
Memories they left behind
when they were made more than mortal*

*Take us in your chariots, too
eggs as old as time
Icarus never flew so high*

*We each have a light inside of us
no matter what's ruined us
This angels Boreal and Wood taught us*

*We bow to the imprisoned angel
Archaeopteryx, your design divine
whom only the giants of old could tame*

Oh yes, there were giants here once.

We'll never fall again

The Deathray Bradburys performed all original material with two notable exceptions – the band often performed heavily sped-up versions of the songs *Come Home*, originally written and performed by the Dave Clark Five (1965), and *Put A Little Love In Your Heart*, originally written and performed by Jackie DeShannon (1968). To date there are two known surviving live bootlegged recordings of the former song, and one live bootlegged recording of the latter. Each of these is included on the Ryko Records reissue of the Deathray Bradburys LP, *There Is A Place*.

Miscellanea

Mark the date, friends: August 31 of our 2000th year:
When finally we free you they will hold us all in their twin warmth.
Eternal Summer is waiting for us.

These songs are yours.
Hold them close.

- liner notes from "There Is A Place" LP

Jimmy knew.
He made angels of the girls.
Better they fly there than die here.
Jimmy knew.
If only he'd been strong enough
to give all of us wings too.

This voice is for Jimmy
One prophet in a black and blind world

We will see you again Jimmy
We will pick starflowers together again.
A bouquet of light we will give to you!

31-08-2000

- from sleeve insert to "Peace-Star For The Lost Sixteen" 7" single

August 31, 2000:

Lucifer Jesus Lords sword and bomb,
they've all abandoned you
When you don't know where to turn

feel us like August in your heart

*Stronger than the tiny history
you've known*

- liner notes to "The Lara Trilogy" 7" single

*Do you need the mighty angel army to fight for you?
Join us, brothers and sisters
The Deathray Bradburys,
your new family
when the world has left you nothing
but pain
and loneliness*

*Our promise runs long and it runs long
We promise you Eternity*

- 31-08-2000 -

- from sleeve insert to "Dark Earth" 7"

*Our rocket
Our holy Egg
leaves in 2000
Be with us, friends
Be freed with us, loved ones
in Windsor, Ontario, Canada*

The reward is everlasting.

They will never hurt you again.

31-08-2000

- jacket copy to Secret Paths To Secret Places (Coordinates) 7"single

69

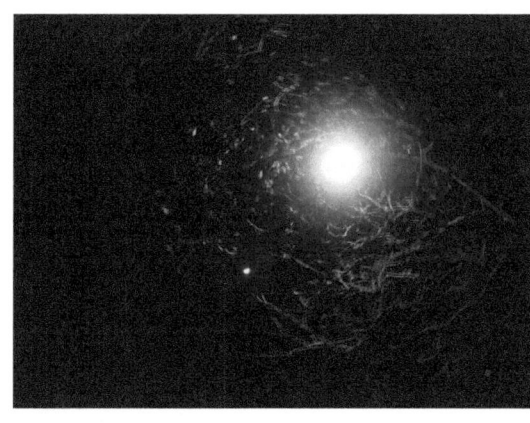

- found written on the wall of a bathroom stall in the Coach And Horses, Windsor, Ontario, Canada, the venue which hosted the Deathray Bradburys' final performance.

About The Author

Alexander Zelenyj was the author of the books *Songs For The Lost, Experiments At 3 Billion A.M.*, and *Black Sunshine*. He lived in Windsor, Ontario, Canada, and was a devout follower of the Deathray Bradburys, compiling this volume circa 2000. He followed the band throughout its tours between 1997 and 2000, and is known to have been present at their final performance. He was one of the 225 fans who disappeared alongside the band in the summer of 2000. His whereabouts remain unknown.

About The Photographer

Elizabeth Walker was the author of the young adult fantasy novel, *She Dreamed Of Dragons*, as well as a variety of zines, most notably 398. She lived in Windsor, Ontario, Canada and, a devout fan of the Deathray Bradburys, followed the band throughout their touring life between the years 1997 – 2000. She documented her travels via numerous photographs, many of which are included in this volume. She was one of the 225 fans who disappeared alongside the Deathray Bradburys following their final performance in the summer of 2000. Her whereabouts remain unknown.

Zelenyj and Walker were the creators of the zine *Un-Prom*.